MONTGOMERY COLLEGE LIBRARY
GERMANTOWN CAMPUS

Religions Ancient and Modern

THE MYTHOLOGY OF ANCIENT
BRITAIN AND IRELAND

RELIGIONS: ANCIENT AND MODERN.

ANIMISM.
By EDWARD CLODD, Author of *The Story of Creation*.

PANTHEISM.
By JAMES ALLANSON PICTON, Author of *The Religion of the Universe*.

THE RELIGIONS OF ANCIENT CHINA.
By Professor GILES, LL.D., Professor of Chinese in the University of Cambridge.

THE RELIGION OF ANCIENT GREECE.
By JANE HARRISON, Lecturer at Newnham College, Cambridge, Author of *Prolegomena to Study of Greek Religion*.

ISLAM.
By AMEER ALI SYED, M.A., C.I.E., late of H.M.'s High Court of Judicature in Bengal, Author of *The Spirit of Islam* and *The Ethics of Islam*.

MAGIC AND FETISHISM.
By Dr. A. C. HADDON, F.R.S., Lecturer on Ethnology at Cambridge University.

THE RELIGION OF ANCIENT EGYPT.
By Professor W. M. FLINDERS PETRIE, F.R.S.

THE RELIGION OF BABYLONIA AND ASSYRIA.
By THEOPHILUS G. PINCHES, late of the British Museum.

EARLY BUDDHISM.
By Professor RHYS DAVIDS, LL.D., late Secretary of The Royal Asiatic Society.

HINDUISM.
By Dr. L. D. BARNETT, of the Department of Oriental Printed Books and MSS., British Museum.

SCANDINAVIAN RELIGION.
By WILLIAM A. CRAIGIE, Joint Editor of the *Oxford English Dictionary*.

CELTIC RELIGION.
By Professor ANWYL, Professor of Welsh at University College, Aberystwyth.

THE MYTHOLOGY OF ANCIENT BRITAIN AND IRELAND.
By CHARLES SQUIRE, Author of *The Mythology of the British Islands*.

JUDAISM
By ISRAEL ABRAHAMS, Lecturer in Talmudic Literature in Cambridge University, Author of *Jewish Life in the Middle Ages*.

THE RELIGION OF ANCIENT ROME.
By CYRIL BAILEY, M.A.

SHINTO, THE ANCIENT RELIGION OF JAPAN.
By W. G. ASTON, C.M.G.

THE RELIGION OF ANCIENT MEXICO AND PERU.
By LEWIS SPENCE, M.A.

EARLY CHRISTIANITY.
By S. B. SLACK, Professor at M'Gill University.

THE PSYCHOLOGICAL ORIGIN AND NATURE OF RELIGION. By Professor J. H. LEUBA.

THE RELIGION OF ANCIENT PALESTINE.
By STANLEY A. COOK.

THE MYTHOLOGY OF ANCIENT BRITAIN AND IRELAND

By
CHARLES SQUIRE
AUTHOR OF
'THE MYTHOLOGY OF THE BRITISH ISLANDS'

FOLCROFT LIBRARY EDITIONS
1973

Library of Congress Cataloging in Publication Data

Squire, Charles.
　The mythology of ancient Britain and Ireland.

　Reprint of the 1909 ed. published by Constable, London.
　Bibliography: p.
　1. Mythology, Celtic.　2. Legends, Celtic.
I. Title.
BL980.G7S6　1973　　　299'.1'6　　　73-13769
ISBN 0-8414-7650-0 (lib. bdg.)

mc 79. 2092

AAA3650

LIMITED 100 COPIES

Manufactured in the United States of America

**FOLCROFT LIBRARY EDITIONS
BOX 182　FOLCROFT, PA. 19032**

THE MYTHOLOGY OF ANCIENT BRITAIN AND IRELAND

By
CHARLES SQUIRE
AUTHOR OF
'THE MYTHOLOGY OF THE BRITISH ISLANDS'

LONDON
CONSTABLE & COMPANY Ltd
10 ORANGE STREET LEICESTER SQUARE
1909

FOREWORD

THIS little book does not profess in any way to supplement the volume upon *Celtic Religion* already contributed to this series. It merely aims at calling the attention of the general reader to the mythology of our own country, that as yet little-known store of Celtic tradition which reflects the religious conceptions of our earliest articulate ancestors. Naturally, its limits compel the writer to dogmatise, or, at most, to touch but very briefly upon disputed points, to ignore many fascinating side-issues, and to refrain from putting forward any suggestions of his own. But he has based his work upon the studies of the leading Celtic scholars, and he believes that the reader may safely accept it as in line with the latest research. C. S.

CONTENTS

CHAP.		PAGE
I.	The Celts and Their Mythology,	1
II.	The Gods of the Continental Celts,	9
III.	The Gods of the Insular Celts,	14
IV.	The Mythical History of Ireland,	31
V.	The Mythical History of Britain,	42
VI.	The Heroic Cycle of Ancient Ulster,	54
VII.	The Fenian, or Ossianic, Sagas,	61
VIII.	The Arthurian Legend,	68
	Chronological Syllabus,	77
	Selected Books bearing on Celtic Mythology,	79

THE MYTHOLOGY OF ANCIENT BRITAIN AND IRELAND

CHAPTER I

THE CELTS AND THEIR MYTHOLOGY

'THE Mythology of Ancient Britain and Ireland.' This title will possibly at first sight suggest to the reader who has been brought up to consider himself essentially an Anglo-Saxon only a few dim memories of Tíw, of Wóden, of Thunor (Thor), and of Fríg, those Saxon deities who have bequeathed to us the names of four of the days of our week.[1] Yet the traces of the *English* gods are comparatively few in Britain, and are not found at all in Ireland, and, at any rate, they can be better studied in the Teutonic countries to which they were native than in this remote outpost of their influence. Preceding the Saxons in Britain by many centuries were the Celts—the 'Ancient Britons'—who themselves possessed a rich mytho-

---

[1] Tíwesdæg, Wódnesdæg, Thunresdæg (later, Thurresdæg), and Frígedæg. Sæter(n)esdæg is adapted from the Latin, *Saturni dies*.

MYTHOLOGY OF ANCIENT BRITAIN

logy, the tradition of which, though obscured, has never been quite lost. In such familiar names as 'Ludgate,' called after a legendary 'good king Lud' who was once the Celtic god Llûdd; in popular folk and fairy tales; in the stories of Arthur and his knights, some of whom are but British divinities in disguise; and in certain of the wilder legends of our early saints, we have fragments of the Celtic mythology handed down tenaciously by Englishmen who had quite as much of the Celt as of the Saxon in their blood.

To what extent the formerly prevalent belief as to the practical extinction of the Celtic inhabitants of our islands at the hands of the Saxons has been reconsidered of late years may be judged from the dictum of one of the most recent students of the subject, Mr. Nicholson, in the preface to his *Keltic Researches*.[1] 'There is good ground to believe,' he says, 'that Lancashire, West Yorkshire, Staffordshire, Worcestershire, Warwickshire, Leicestershire, Rutland, Cambridgeshire, Wiltshire, Somerset, and part of Sussex, are as Keltic as Perthshire and North Munster; that Cheshire, Shropshire, Herefordshire, Monmouth-

---

[1] *Keltic Researches: Studies in the History and Distribution of the Ancient Goidelic Language and Peoples*, by Edward Williams Byron Nicholson, M A.; London, 1904.

shire, Gloucestershire, Devon, Dorset, Northamptonshire, Huntingdonshire, and Bedfordshire are more so—and equal to North Wales and Leinster; while Buckinghamshire and Hertfordshire exceed even this degree and are on a level with South Wales and Ulster. Cornwall, of course, is more Keltic than any other English county, and as much so as Argyll, Inverness-shire, or Connaught.' If these statements are well founded, Celt and Teuton must be very equally woven into the fabric of the British nation.

But even the Celts themselves were not the first inhabitants of our islands. Their earliest arrivals found men already in possession. We meet with their relics in the 'long barrows,' and deduce from them a short, dark, long-skulled race of slight physique and in a relatively low stage of civilisation. Its origin is uncertain, and so is all we think we know of it, and, though it must have greatly influenced Aryan-Celtic custom and myth, it would be hard to put a finger definitely upon any point where the two different cultures have met and blended.

We know more about its conquerors. According to the most generally accepted theory, there were two main streams of Aryan emigration from the Continent into a non-Aryan Britain, both belonging to the same linguistic branch of the Indo-European stock—the Celtic—but speaking variant dialects of that tongue—Goidelic, or Gaelic, and Brythonic, or British. Of these the Goidels were the earlier, their first settlers having arrived at some period between 1000 and 500 B.C., while the Brythons, or Brĭttŏnes, seem to have appeared about the third century B.C., steadily encroaching upon and ousting their forerunners. With the Brythons must be considered the Belgæ, who made, still later, an extensive invasion of Southern Britain, but who seem to have been eventually assimilated to, or absorbed in, the Brythons, to whom they were, at any rate linguistically, much akin.[1] In physique, as well as in language, there was probably a difference between the Brythons and the Goidels, the latter containing some admixture of the broad-headed stock of Central Europe, and it is thought also that the Goidels must have become in course of time modified by admixture with the dark, long-skulled non-Aryan race. The Romans appear to have recognised more than one type in Britain, distinguishing between the inhabitants of the coast regions

---

[1] Rhŷs, *Celtic Britain*, 1904, and Rhŷs and Brynmor-Jones, *The Welsh People*, 1906.

nearest to France, who resembled the Gauls, and the ruddy-haired, large-limbed natives of the North, who seemed to them more akin to the Germans. To these may be added certain people of West Britain, whose dark complexions and curly hair caused Tacitus to regard them as immigrants from Spain, and who probably belonged either wholly or largely to the aboriginal stock.[1]

We have no records of the clash and counter-clash of savage warfare which must, if this theory be taken as correct, have marked, first, the conquest of the aborigines by the Goidels, and afterwards the displacement of the Goidels by the later branches of the Celts. Nor do we know when or how the Goidels crossed from Britain to Ireland. All that we can state with approximate certainty is that at the time of the Roman domination the Brythons were in possession of all Britain south of the Tweed, with the exception of the extreme West, while the Goidels had most of Ireland, the Isle of Man, Cumberland, North and South Wales, Cornwall, and Devon, as well as, in the opinion of some authorities, the West Highlands of Scotland,[2] the primitive dark

---

[1] Tacitus, *Agricola*, chap. xi.
[2] It is, however, held by others that the Goidels of Scotland did not reach that country (from Ireland) before the Christian era.

race being still found in certain portions of Ireland and of West Britain, and in Scotland north of the Grampian Hills.

It is the beliefs, traditions, and legends of these Goidels and Brythons, and their more unmixed descendants, the modern Gaels and Cymry, which make up our mythology. Nor is the stock of them by any means so scanty as the remoteness and obscurity of the age in which they were still vital will probably have led the reader to expect. We can gather them from six different sources: (1) Dedications to Celtic divinities upon altars and votive tablets, large numbers of which have been found both on the Continent and in our own islands; (2) Irish, Scottish, and Welsh manuscripts which, though they date only from mediaeval times, contain, copied from older documents, legends preserved from the pagan age; (3) So-called histories — notably that of Geoffrey of Monmouth, written in the twelfth century— which consist largely of mythical matter disguised as a record of the ancient British kings; (4) Early hagiology, in which the myths of gods of the pagan Goidels and Brythons have been taken over by the ecclesiasts and fathered upon the patron saints of the Celtic Church; (5) The groundwork of British bardic tradition upon

THE CELTS AND THEIR MYTHOLOGY

which the Welsh, Breton, and Norman minstrels, and, following them, the romance-writers of all the more civilised European countries founded the Arthurian cycle; (6) And lastly, upon folk tales which, although but lately reduced to writing, are probably as old, or even older, than any of the other sources.

A few lines must here be spared to show the reader the nature of the mediaeval manuscripts just mentioned. They consist of larger or smaller vellum or parchment volumes, into which the scribe of a great family or of a monastery laboriously copied whatever lore, godly or worldly, was deemed most worthy of perpetuation. They thus contain very varied matter:—portions of the Bible; lives of saints and works attributed to them; genealogies and learned treatises; as well as the poems of the bards and the legends of tribal heroes who had been the gods of an earlier age. The most famous of them are, in Irish, the Books of the Dun Cow, of Leinster, of Lecan, of Ballymote, and the Yellow Book of Lecan; and in Welsh, the so-called 'Four Ancient Books of Wales'—the Black Book of Carmarthen, the Book of Aneurin, the Book of Taliesin, and the Red Book of Hergest—together with the White Book of Rhydderch. Taken as a whole, they date from the beginning of the twelfth century to the end of the sixteenth; the oldest being the Book of the Dun Cow, the compiler of which died in the year 1106. But much of their substance is far older—can, indeed, be proved to ante-date the seventh century—while the mythical tales and poems must, even at this earlier age, have long been traditional. They preserve for us, in however distorted a form, much of the legendary lore of the Celts.

The Irish manuscripts have suffered less sophistication than the Welsh. In them the gods still appear as divine and the heroes as the pagans they were; while their Welsh congeners pose as kings or knights, or even as dignitaries of the Christian Church. But the more primitive, less adulterated, Irish myths can be brought to throw light upon the Welsh, and thus their accretions can be stripped from them till they appear in their true guise. In this way scholarship is gradually unveiling a mythology whose appeal is not merely to our patriotism. In itself it is often poetic and lofty, and, in its disguise of Arthurian romance, it has influenced modern art and literature only less potently than that mighty inspiration—the mythology of Ancient Greece.

CHAPTER II

THE GODS OF THE CONTINENTAL CELTS

But before approaching the myths of the Celts of Great Britain and Ireland, we must briefly glance at the mythology of the Celts of Continental Europe, that Gallia from which Goidels and Brythons alike came. From the point of view of literature the subject is barren; for whatever mythical and heroic legends the Gauls once had have perished. But there have been brought to light a very large number not only of dedicatory inscriptions to, but also of statues and bas-reliefs of, the ancient gods of Gaul. And, to afford us some clue amid their bewildering variety, a certain amount of information is given us by classic writers, especially by Julius Caesar in his Commentaries on the Gallic War.

He mentions five chief divinities of the Gauls, apparently in the order of their reputed power. First of all, he says, they worship Mercury, as inventor of the arts and patron of travellers and merchants. Next comes Apollo, the divine healer, and he is followed by Minerva, the teacher of useful trades, by Jupiter, who rules the sky, and by Mars, the director of battles.[1] This does not, of course, mean that Caesar considered the gods of the Gauls to be exactly those of the Romans, but that imaginary beings represented as carrying out much the same functions as the Roman Mercury, Apollo, Minerva, Jupiter, and Mars were worshipped by them. In practice, too, the Romans readily assimilated the deities of conquered peoples to their own; hence it is that in the inscriptions discovered in Gaul, and indeed in our own islands, we find the names of Celtic divinities preceded by those of the Roman gods they were considered to resemble:—as Mercurius Artaios, Apollo Grannos, Minerva Belĭsăma, Jupiter Sŭcellos, and Mars Cămŭlos.

Modern discoveries quite bear out Caesar's statement as to the importance to the Gaulish mind of the god whom he called Mercury. Numerous place-names attest it in modern France. Costly statues stood in his honour; one, of massive silver, was dug up in the gardens of the Luxembourg, while another, made in bronze by a Greek artist for the great temple of the

[1] *De Bello Gallico*, iv. 17.

THE GODS OF THE CONTINENTAL CELTS

Arverni upon the summit of the Puy de Dôme, is said to have stood a hundred and twenty feet high, and to have taken ten years to finish. Yet it would seem to have been rather for the war-god that some at least of the warlike Gauls reserved their chief worship. The regard in which he was held is proved by two of his names or titles:—Rīgĭsămos ('Most Royal,') and Albiŏrix ('King of the World'). Much honour, too, must have been paid to a Gaulish Apollo, Grannos, lord of healing waters, from whom Aix-la-Chapelle (anciently called Aquae Granni), Graux and Eaux Graunnes, in the Vosges, and Granheim, in Würtemburg, took their names, for we are told by Dion Cassius [1] that the Roman Emperor Caracalla invoked him as the equal of the better-known Aesculapius and Serapis. Another Gaulish 'Apollo,' Toutiŏrix ('Lord of the People') has won, however, a far wider, if somewhat vicarious fame. Accidentally confounded with Theodoric the Goth, his mythical achievements are, in all probability, responsible for the wilder legends connected with that historical hero under his title of Dietrich von Bern.[2]

But the gods of the Continental Celts are being

[1] lxxvii. 15.
[2] Rhŷs, *Hibbert Lectures* for 1886, pp. 30-32.

treated in this series[1] far more competently than is in the power of the present writer. For his purpose and his readers', the only Gaulish deities who need be noticed here are some whose names reappear in the written myths of our own Islands.

In the oldest Irish and Welsh manuscripts we meet with personages whose names and attributes identify them with divinities whom we know to have been worshipped in the Celtic world abroad. Ogma combines in Gaelic mythology the characters of the god of eloquence and poetry and the professional champion of his circle, the Tuatha Dé Danann, while a second-century Greek writer called Lucian describes a Gaulish Ogmïos, who, though he was represented as armed with the club and lion-skin of Heracles, was yet considered the exponent of persuasive speech. He was depicted as drawing men after him by golden cords attached from his tongue to their ears and, as the 'old man eloquent,' whose varied experience made his words worth listening to, he was shown as wrinkled and bald. Altogether (as a native assured Lucian), he taught that true power resides in wise words as much as in doughty deeds, a lesson

[1] *Celtic Religion*, by Professor E. Anwyl, to whom the writer here takes the opportunity of gratefully acknowledging his indebtedness for valuable help towards the making of this book.

THE GODS OF THE CONTINENTAL CELTS

not yet quite forgotten by the Celt.[1] In the Continental Lŭgus, whose name still clings to the cities of Lyons, Laon, and Leyden, all anciently called Lŭgŭdūnum ('Lŭgus's town'), we may claim to see that important figure of the Goidelic legends, Lug of the Long Hand. With the Gaulish goddess Brĭgindu, of whom mention is made in a dedicatory tablet found at Volnay, near Beaune, we may connect Brigit, the Irish Minerva or Vesta who passed down into saintship as Saint Bridget. The war-god[2] Cămŭlos is possibly found in Ireland as Cumhal (*Coul*), father of the famous Finn; in Belīnus, an apocryphal British king who reappears in romance as Balin of the *Morte Darthur*, we probably have the Gaulish Bĕlĕnos, whom the Latin writer Ausonius mentions as a sun-god served by Druids; while Măpŏnos, identified by the Romans with Apollo, we find in the Welsh stories as Mabon son of Modron (Mātrŏna), a companion of Arthur.

It is by a curious irony that we must now look for the stories of Celtic gods to two islands once considered so remote and uncivilised as hardly to belong to the Celtic world at all.

[1] Rhŷs, *Hibbert Lectures*, pp. 13-20.
[2] Cămŭlus seems to have been a more important god than his Roman equation with Mars (p. 10) suggests. Professor Rhŷs calls him a 'Mars-Jupiter.' Cf. pp. 11, 20-21, and 63 of this book.

CHAPTER III

THE GODS OF THE INSULAR CELTS

It would be impossible, in so small a space as we can afford, to mention all, or indeed any but a few, of the swarming deities of ancient Britain and Ireland, most of them, in all probability, extremely local in their nature. The best we can do is to look for a fixed point, and this we find in certain gods whose names and attributes are very largely common to both the Goidels and the Brythons. In the old Gaelic literature they are called the Tuatha Dé Danann (*Tooăhu dae donann*), the 'Tribe of the Goddess Danu,' and in the Welsh documents, the 'Children of Dôn' and the 'Children of Llŷr.'

Danu—or Donu, as the name is sometimes spelt—seems to have been considered by the Goidels as the ancestress of the gods, who collectively took their title from her. We also find mention of another ancient female deity of some-

THE GODS OF THE INSULAR CELTS

what similar name, Anu or Ana, worshipped in Munster as a goddess of prosperity and abundance,[1] who was likewise described as the mother of the Irish Pantheon—'Well she used to cherish the gods,' wrote a commentator on a ninth-century Irish glossary.[2] Turning to the British mythology, we find that some of the principal figures in what seems to be its oldest stratum are called sons or daughters of Dôn: Gwydion son of Dôn; Govannon son of Dôn; Arianrod daughter of Dôn. But Arianrod is also termed the daughter of Beli, which makes it reasonably probable that Beli, who otherwise appears as a mythical king of the Brythons, was considered to be Dôn's consort. His Gaelic counterpart is perhaps Bilé, the ancestor of the Milesians, the first Celtic settlers in Ireland, and though Bilé is nowhere connected with Danu in the scattered myths which have come down to us, the analogy is suggestive. Bilé and Beli seem to represent on Gaelic and British soil respectively the Dis Pater from whom Caesar[3] tells us the Gauls believed themselves to be descended, the two

[1] *Coir Anmann.* 'The Choice of Names.' Translated by Dr. Whitley Stokes in *Irische Texte.*
[2] Cormac's *Glossary.* Translated by O'Donovan and edited by Stokes.
[3] *De Bello Gallico,* vi. 18.

shadowy pairs, Bilé and Danu, Beli and Dôn, standing for the divine Father and Mother alike of gods and men.

Llŷr, the head of the other family, appears in Gaelic myths as Lêr (*gen.* Lir), both names probably meaning 'the Sea.' Though ranked among the Tuatha Dé Danann, Lêr seems to descend from a different line, and plays little part in the stories of the earlier history of the Irish gods, though he is prominent in what are perhaps equally ancient legends concerning Finn and the Fenians. On the other hand, there are details concerning the British Llŷr which suggest that he may have been borrowed by the Brythons from the Goidels. His wife is called Iwerydd (Ireland), and he himself is termed Llŷr Llediaith, *i.e.* 'Llŷr of the Half-Tongue,' which is supposed to mean that his language could be but imperfectly understood. He gave its name to Leicester, originally Llŷr-cestre, called in Welsh Caer Lyr, while, through Geoffrey of Monmouth, he has become Shakespeare's 'King Lear,' and is found in hagiology as the head of the first of the 'Three Chief Holy Families of the Isle of Britain.'

Both Lêr and Llŷr are, however, better known to mythology by their sons than from their own exploits. We find the Gaelic Bron mac Lir and Manannán mac Lir paralleling the British Brân ab Llŷr and Manawyddan ab Llŷr. Of the Irish Bron we know nothing, except that he gave his name to a place called Mag Bron ('Bron's Plain'), but Brân is one of the most clearly outlined figures in the Brythonic mythology. He is represented as of gigantic size—no house or ship which was ever made could contain him in it—and, when he laid himself down across a river, an army could march over him as though upon a bridge. He was the patron of minstrelsy and bardism, and claimed, according to a mediaeval poem[1] put into the mouth of the sixth-century Welsh poet Taliesin, to be himself a bard, a harper, a player upon the *crûth*, and seven score other musicians all at once. He is a king in Hades with whom the sons of Dôn fight to obtain the treasures of the Underworld, and, paradoxically enough, has passed down into ecclesiastical legend as 'the Blessed Brân,' who brought Christianity from Rome to Britain.

Turning to the brothers of Bron and Brân, it is of the Irish god this time that we have the fullest account. Manannán mac Lir has always

[1] 'Book of Taliesin,' poem xlviii., in Skene's *Four Ancient Books of Wales*, vol. i. p. 297.

been one of the most vivid of the figures of the Tuatha Dé Danann. Clad in his invulnerable mail, with jewelled helmet which flashed like the sun, robed in his cloak of invisibility woven from the fleeces of the flocks of Paradise, and girt with his sword 'Retaliator' which never failed to slay; whether riding upon his horse 'Splendid Mane,' which went swift as the spring wind over land or sea, or voyaging in his boat 'Wave-Sweeper,' which needed neither sail nor oar nor rudder, he presents as striking a picture as can be found in any mythology. The especial patron of sailors, he was invoked by them as 'The Lord of Headlands,' while the merchants claimed that he was the founder of their guild. He was connected especially with the Isle of Man; euhemerising legend asserts that he was its first king, and his grave, which is thirty yards long, is still pointed out at Peel Castle. A curious tradition credits him with three legs, and it is these limbs, arranged like the spokes of a wheel, which appear on the arms of the Island. His British analogue, Manawyddan, can be seen less clearly through the mists of myth. On the one hand he appears as a kind of culture-hero—hunter, craftsman, and agriculturist; while on the other he is the enemy of those gods who seem most beneficent to man.

THE GODS OF THE INSULAR CELTS

One of his achievements was the building, in the peninsula of Gower, of the Fortress of Oeth and Annoeth, which is described as a gruesome prison made of human bones; and in it he is said to have incarcerated no less a person than the famous Arthur.

Whether or not we may take the children of Llŷr to have been gods of the sea, we can hardly go wrong in considering the children of Dôn as having come to be regarded as deities of the sky. Constellations bore their names — Cassiopeia's Chair was called Dôn's Court (*Llys Dôn*), the Northern Crown, Arianrod's Castle (*Caer Arianrod*), and the Milky Way, the Castle of Gwydion (*Caer Gwydion*). Taken as a whole, they do not present such close analogies to the Irish Tuatha Dé Danann as do the Children of Llyr. Nevertheless, there are striking parallels extending to what would seem to have been some of the greatest of their gods. In Irish myth we find Nuada Argetlám, and in British, Nûdd, or Llûdd Llaw Ereint, both epithets having the same meaning of the 'Silver Hand.' What it signified we do not know; in Irish literature there is a lame story to account for it (see p. 35), but if there was a kindred British version it has been lost. But the attributes of both Nuada and Nûdd

MYTHOLOGY OF ANCIENT BRITAIN

(Llûdd) show them as the kind of deity whom the Romans would have equated with their Jupiter. Nuada rules over the Tuatha Dé Danann, while Llûdd, or Nûdd, appears as a mythical British king, who changed the name of his favourite city from Trinovantum (Geoffrey's 'New Troy') to Caer Ludd, which afterwards became London. He is said to have been buried at Ludgate, a legend which we may perhaps connect with the tradition that a temple of the Britons formerly occupied the site of St. Paul's. However this may be, we know that he was worshipped at Lydney in Gloucestershire, for the ruins of his sanctuary have been discovered there, with varied inscriptions to him as DEVO NODENTI, D.M. NODONTI, and DEO NUDENTE M., as well as a small plaque of bronze, probably representing him, which shows us a youthful figure, with head surrounded by solar rays, standing in a four-horse chariot, and attended by two winged genii and two Tritons.[1] The 'M' of the inscription may have read in full MAGNO, MAXIMO, or, more probably,[2] MARTI, which would be the Roman, or Romano-British, way of describing the god as the

[1] A monograph on the subject, entitled *Roman Antiquities at Lydney Park, Gloucestershire*, by the Rev. W. H. Bathurst, was published in 1879.
[2] Professor Rhŷs, following Dr. Hübner.

THE GODS OF THE INSULAR CELTS

warrior he appears as in Irish legend. With him, though not necessarily as his consort, we must rank a goddess of war whose name, Mórrígu (the 'Great Queen'), attests her importance, and who may have been the same as Macha ('Battle'), Badb ('Carrion Crow'), and Nemon ('Venomous'), whose name suggests comparison with the British Nĕmĕtŏna,[1] a war-goddess to whom an inscription has been found at Bath. The wife of Llûdd, however, in Welsh myth is called Gwyar, but *her* name also implies fighting, for it means 'gore.'[2] The children of both the Gaelic and the British god play noteworthy parts in Celtic legend. Tadg (*Teague*), son of Nuada, was the grandfather, upon his mother's side, of the famous Finn mac Coul. Gwyn, son of Nûdd, originally a deity of the Underworld, has passed down into living folk-lore as king of the *Tylwyth Teg*, the Welsh fairies.

Another of the sons of Dôn whom we also find in the ranks of the Tuatha Dé Danann is the god of Smith-craft, Govannon,[3] in Irish Goibniu (*gen.* Goibnenn). The Gaelic deity appears in

[1] The two are identified by the French scholar, M. Gaidoz, but the equation is not everywhere upheld.

[2] Rhŷs, *Studies in the Arthurian Legend*, p. 169.

[3] Also called in Welsh, 'Govynion Hên.' *Hên* means 'The Ancient.'

mythical literature as the forger of the weapons of his divine companions and the brewer of an ale of immortality; and in folk-tales as the Gobhan Saer, the fairy architect to whom popular fancy has attributed the round towers and the early churches of Ireland. Of his British analogue we know less, but he is found, in company with his brother Amaethon, the god of Husbandry, engaging in a wonderful feat of agriculture at the bidding of Arthur.

But, greater than any of the other sons of Dôn would seem to have been Gwydion, who appears in British myth as a 'Culture-Hero,' the teacher of arts and giver of gifts to his fellows. His name and attributes have caused more than one leading mythologist to conjecture whether he may not have been identical with a still greater figure, the Teutonic Woden, or Odin. Professor Rhŷs, especially, has drawn, in his *Hibbert Lectures* (1886) on Celtic Heathendom, a remarkable series of parallels between the two characters, as they are figured respectively in Celtic and Teutonic myth.[1] Both were alike pre-eminent in war-craft and in the arts of story-telling, poetry, and magic, and both gained through painful experiences the lore which they placed

[1] Pp. 282-304.

THE GODS OF THE INSULAR CELTS

at the service of mankind. This is represented on the Celtic side by the poetical inspiration which Gwydion acquired through his sufferings while in the power of the gods of Hades, and in Teutonic story by two draughts of wisdom, one which Woden obtained by guile from Gundfled, daughter of the giant Suptung, and another which he could only get by pledging one of his eyes to its owner Sokk-mimi, the Giant of the Abyss. Each was born of a mysterious, little-known father and mother; each had a love whose name was associated with a symbolic wheel, who posed as a maiden and was furiously indignant at the birth of her children; and each lost his son[1] in a curiously similar fashion, and sought for him sorrowfully to bring him back to the world. Still more striking are the strange myths which tell how each of them could create human out of vegetable life; Woden made a man and a woman out of trees, while Gwydion 'enchanted a woman from blossoms' as a bride for Lleu, on whom his unnatural mother had 'laid a destiny' that he should never have a wife of the people of this earth. But the equation, fascinating though it is, is much discounted by the fact that the only traces we find of

[1] But see note 2 on following page.

MYTHOLOGY OF ANCIENT BRITAIN

Gwydion in Britain are a few stories connected with certain place-names in the Welsh counties of Carnarvonshire and Merionethshire. This would seem to suggest that, like so many of the divine figures of the Celts, his fame was merely a local one, and that he is more likely to have been simply the 'lord of Mona and Arvon,' as a Welsh bard calls him, than so great a deity as the Teutonic god he at first sight seems to resemble. His nearest Celtic equivalents we may find in the Gaulish Ogmïos, figured as a Heracles who won his way by persuasion rather than by force, and the Gaelic Ogma, at once champion of the Tuatha Dé Danann, god of Literature and Eloquence, and inventor of the ogam alphabet.

It is another of the family of Dôn—Arianrod, the goddess of the constellation 'Corona Borealis,' to which she sometime gave her name, which was popularly interpreted as 'Silver Wheel,'[1] who appears in connection with Gwydion as the mother of Lleu, or Llew, depicted as the helper of his uncles, Gwydion[2] and Amaethon,

[1] The form Arianrod, in earlier Welsh Aranrot, may have been evolved by popular etymology under the influence of *arian* (silver).

[2] Lleu is sometimes treated as the *son* of Gwydion and Arianrod, though there is no direct statement to this effect in Welsh literature, and the point has been elaborated by Professor Rhŷs mainly on the analogy of similar Celtic myths. The fact,

in their battles against the powers of the Underworld. Llew's epithet is *Llaw Gyffes*, *i.e.* 'Of the (?) Firm Hand,' with which we may compare that of *Lámfada* ('Of the Long Hand') borne by the Goidelic deity Lugh, or Lug. This tempts us to regard the two mythical figures as identical, equating Lleu (Llew) also with the Gaulish Lŭgus. There are, however, considerable difficulties in the way. Phonologically, the word *Lleu* or *Llew* cannot be the exact equivalent of *Lŭgus*, while the restricted character of the place-names and legends connected with Lleu as a mythic figure mark him as belonging to much the same circle of local tradition as Gwydion. Nor do we know enough about Lleu to be able to make any large comparison between him and the Irish Lug. They are alike in the meaning of their epithets, in their rapid growth after birth, and in their helping the more beneficent gods against their enemies. But any such details are wanting with regard to Lleu as those which make the Irish god so clear-cut and picturesque a figure. Such was the radiance of Lug's face that

however, that Lleu is found in genealogies as ' Louhé (Lou Hên), son of Guitgé' (the 'Gwydyen' of the Book of Aneurin and the Book of Taliesin), seems to show that the idea was not absolutely unfamiliar to the Welsh. For another side of the question see chap. ii. of *The Welsh People* (Rhŷs and Brynmor-Jones).

it seemed like the sun, and none could gaze steadily at it. He was the acknowledged master of all arts, both of war and of peace. Among his possessions were a magic spear which slew of itself, and a hound of most wonderful qualities. His rod-sling was seen in heaven as the rainbow, and the Milky Way was called 'Lug's chain.' First accepted as the sun-god of the Goidels, it is now more usual to regard him as a personification of fire. There is, however, evidence to show that a certain amount of confusion between the two great sources of light and heat is a not unnatural phenomenon of the myth-making mind.[1]

This similarity in name, title, and attributes between Bilé and Beli, Danu and Dôn, Lêr and Llŷr, Bron and Brân, Manannán and Manawyddan, Nuada and Nûdd (or Llûdd), (?) Nemon and Někětǒna, Govannon and Goibniu, and (?) Lug and Lleu has suggested to several competent scholars that the Brythons received them from the other branch of the Celts, either by inheritance from the Goidels in Britain or by direct borrowing from the Goidels of Ireland. But such a case has not yet been made out convincingly, nor is it necessary in order to account

[1] The Rig-Veda, for instance, tells us that 'Agni (Fire) is Sûrya (the Sun) in the morning, Sûrya is Agni at night.'

THE GODS OF THE INSULAR CELTS

for similar names and myths among kindred races of the same stock. Whatever may be the explanation of their likeness, these names are, after all, but a few taken out of two long lists of divine characters. Naturally, too, deities whose attributes are alike appear under different names in the myths of the two branches of the Celts. Specialised gods could have been but few in type; while their names might vary with every tribe. Some of these it may be interesting to compare briefly, as we have already done in the case of the British Gwydion and the Gaelic Ogma. The Irish Dagda, whose name (from an earlier Dagodêvos), would seem to have meant the 'good god,' whose cauldron, called the 'Undry,' fed all the races of the earth, and who played the seasons into being with his mystic harp, may be compared with Dôn's brother, the wise and just Mâth, who is represented as a great magician who teaches his lore to his nephew Gwydion. Angus, one of the Dagda's sons, whose music caused all who heard to follow it, and whose kisses became birds which sang of love, would be, as a divinity of the tender passion, a counterpart of Dwyn, or Dwynwen,[1] the British Venus,

[1] Dwynwen means 'the Blessed Dwyn.' The church of this goddess-saint is Llanddwyn in Anglesey.

who was, even by the later Welsh bards, hymned as the 'saint of love.' Brigit, the Dagda's daughter, patroness of poetry, may find her analogue in the Welsh Kerridwen, the owner of a 'cauldron of Inspiration and Science.' Diancecht (*Dianket*) the Goidelic god of Healing seems to have no certain equivalent in Brythonic myth, but Mider, a deity of the Underworld—though his name would bring him rather into line with the British Medyr, who, however, appears in Welsh romance only as a wonderful marksman—may be here considered in connection with Pwyll, the hero of a legendary cycle apparently local to Dyved (the Roman province of Demetia, and, roughly, south-west Wales). Pwyll, who may perhaps represent the same god as the Arawn who is connected with him in mythic romance, appears as an Underworld deity, friendly with the children of Llyr and opposed to the sons of Dôn, and with him are grouped his wife, Rhiannon (in older Celtic Rĭgantŏna, or 'Great Queen') and his son Prydéri, who succeeds his father as king of Annwn or Annwvn (the British Other World), jointly with Manawyddan son of Llŷr. He is represented as the antagonist of Gwydion, who is eventually his conqueror and slayer.

But even the briefest account of the Celtic

THE GODS OF THE INSULAR CELTS

gods would be incomplete without some mention of a second group of figures of British legend, some of whom may have owed their names to history, with which local myths became incorporated. These are the characters of early Welsh tradition who appear afterwards as the kings and knights and ladies of mediaeval Arthurian romance. There is Arthur himself, half god, half king, with his queen Gwenhwyvar—whose father, Tennyson's 'Leodogran, the King of Cameliard,' was the giant Ogyrvan, patron and perhaps originator of bardism—and Gwalchmai and Medrawt, who, though they are usually called his nephews, seem in older story to have been considered his sons. A greater figure in some respects even than Arthur must have been Myrddin, a mythical personage doubtless to be distinguished from his namesake the supposed sixth-century bard to whom are attributed the poems in the Black Book of Carmarthen. Prominent, too, are Urien, who sometimes appears as a powerful prince in North Britain, and sometimes as a deity with similar attributes to those of Brân, the son of Llŷr, and Kai, who may have been (as seems likely from a passage in the *Mabinogion* story of 'Kulhwch and Olwen') a personification of fire, or the mortal chieftain with whom tradition has associated Caer Gai in Merionethshire and Cai Hir in Glamorganshire. Connected, too, by a loose thread with Arthur's story are the figures of what is thought to have been the independant mythic cycle of March (King Mark), his queen Essyllt (Iseult), and his nephew Drystan, or Trystan, (Sir Tristrem). All these, and many others, seem to be inhabitants of an obscure borderland where vanishing myth and doubtful history have mingled.

The memory of this cycle has passed down into living folk-lore among the descendants of those Brythons who, fleeing from the Saxon conquerors, found new homes upon the other side of the English Channel. Little Britain has joined with Great Britain in cherishing the fame of Arthur, while Myrddin (in Breton, Marzin), described as the master of all knowledge, owner of all wealth, and lord of Fairyland, can only be the folk-lore representative of a once great deity. These two stand out clearly; while the other characters of the Brythonic mythology have lost their individualities, to merge into the nameless hosts of the dwarfs (*Korred*), the fairies (*Korrigan*), and the water-spirits (*Morgan*) of Breton popular belief.

CHAPTER IV

THE MYTHICAL HISTORY OF IRELAND

According to the early monkish annalists, who sought to nullify the pagan traditions against which they fought by turning them into a pseudo-history, Ireland was first inhabited by a lady named Cessair and her followers, shortly after the flood. They describe her as a grand-daughter of Noah; but it is more likely that she represented a tribal goddess or divine ancestress of the pre-Celtic people in Ireland.[1] Whoever she may have been, her influence was not lasting. She perished, with all her race, leaving a free field to her successors.

We say 'field' with intention; for Ireland consisted then of only one plain, treeless and grassless, but watered by three lakes and nine rivers. The race that succeeded Cessair, however, soon set to work to remedy this. Partholon, who

[1] Rhŷs, *Celtic Britain*, Third edition, p. 288.

landed with twenty-four males and twenty-four females upon the first of May (the Celtic feast of 'Beltaine'), enlarged the island to four plains with seven new lakes. The newcomers themselves also increased and multiplied, so that in three centuries their original forty-eight members had become five thousand. But, on the three hundredth anniversary of their coming, an epidemic sprang up which annihilated them. They gathered together upon the original first-created plain to die, and the place of their funeral is still marked by the mound of Tallaght, near Dublin.

Before these early colonists, Ireland had been inhabited by a race of demons or giants, described as monstrous in size and hideous in shape, many of them being footless and handless, while others had the heads of animals. Their name *Fomor*, which means 'under wave,'[1] and their descent from a goddess named Domnu, or 'the Deep,'[2] seem to show them as a personification of the sea waves. To the Celtic mind the sea represented darkness and death, and the *Fomorach* appear as the antithesis of the beneficent gods of light and life. Partholon and his people had to fight them for a foothold in Ireland, and did so successfully.

[1] Rhŷs, *Hibbert Lectures*, p. 591.
[2] *Ibid.*, p. 598.

THE MYTHICAL HISTORY OF IRELAND

The next immigrants were less fortunate. The People of Nemed followed the Race of Partholon, and added twelve new plains and four more lakes to Ireland. But, after being scourged by a similar epidemic to that which had destroyed their forerunners, they found themselves at the mercy of the Fomorach, who ordered them to deliver up as tribute two-thirds of the children born to them in every year. In desperation they attacked the stronghold of the giants upon Tory Island, off the coast of Donegal, and took it, slaying Conann, one of the Fomor Kings, with many of his followers. But Morc, the other king, terribly avenged this defeat, and the Nemedians, reduced to a handful of thirty, took ship and fled the country.

A new race now came into possession, and here we seem to find ourselves upon historical ground, however uncertain. These were three tribes called *Fir Domnann*, the 'Men of Domnu,' *Fir Gailióin*, the 'Men of Gailióin' and *Fir Bolg*, the 'Men of Bolg,' emigrants, according to the annalists, from Greece. They are generally considered as having represented to the Gaelic mind the pre-Celtic inhabitants of Ireland, and the fact that their principal tribe was called the 'Men of Domnu' suggests that the Fomorach, who are called 'Gods of Domnu,' may have been the divinities of their worship. At any rate, we never find them in conflict, like the other races, with the gigantic and demoniac powers. On the contrary, they themselves and the Fomorach alike struggle against, and are conquered by, the next people to arrive.

These are the Tuatha Dé Danann, in whom all serious students now recognise the gods of the Celts in Ireland, and who, as we have seen, parallel the earlier divinities of the Celts in Britain. They are variously fabled to have come from the sky, or else from the north or the south of the world. Wherever they came from, they landed in Ireland upon the same mystic First of May, bringing with them their four chief treasures —Nuada's sword, whose blow needed no second, Lug's living lance, which required no hand to wield it in battle, the Dagda's cauldron, whose supply of food never failed, and the mysterious 'Stone of Destiny,' which would cry out with a human voice to acclaim a rightful king. This stone is said by some to be identical with our own 'Coronation Stone' at Westminster, which was brought from Scone by Edward I., but it is more probable that it still stands upon the hill of Tara, where it was preserved as a kind of fetish by the early kings of Ireland.[1] They had not been long

[1] See *The Coronation Stone*. A monograph by W. F. Skene.

in occupation of the country before their presence was discovered by the race in possession. After some parleying and offers to partition the island, a battle, known as that of Moytura—in Irish *Mag Tuireadh*, 'Plain of the Pillars'—was fought near Cong, in Mayo, in which the Tuatha Dé Danann gained the victory. Handing over the province of Connaught to the conquered race, they took possession of the rest of Ireland, fixing their capital at the historic Tara, then called Drumcain.

Their conquest, however, still left them with a powerful enemy to face, for the Fomorach were by no means ready to accept their occupation of the soil. But the Tuatha Dé Danann thought to find a means of conciliating those hostile powers. Their own king, Nuada, had lost his right hand in the battle of Moytura, and, although it had been replaced by an artifical one of silver, he had, according to the Celtic law which forbade a blemished person to sit upon the throne, been obliged to renounce the sovereignty. They therefore sent to Elathan, King of the Fomorach, inviting his son Bress to ally himself with them, and become their ruler. This was agreed to; and a marriage was made between Bress and Brigit the daughter of the Dagda, while Cian, a son of Diancecht the god of Medicine, wedded Ethniu, the daughter of a powerful prince of the Fomorach named Balor.

But Bress soon showed himself in his true Fomorian colours. He put excessive taxes upon his new subjects, and seized for himself the control of all the necessities of life, so that the proud gods were forced to manual labour to obtain food and warmth. Worse than this even — to the Gaelic mind — he hoarded all he got, spending none of his wealth in free feasts and public entertainments. But at last he put a personal affront upon Cairbré son of Ogma, the principal bard of the Tuatha Dé Danann, who retorted with a satire so scathing that boils broke out upon its victim's face. Thus Bress himself became blemished, and was obliged to abdicate, and Nuada, whose lost hand had meanwhile been replaced by the spells and medicaments of a son and daughter of Diancecht, came forward again to take the Kingship. Bress returned to his undersea home, and, at a council of the Fomorach, it was decided to make war upon the Tuatha Dé Danann, and drive them out of Ireland.

But now a mighty help was coming to the gods. From the marriage of Diancecht's son and Balor's daughter was born a child called Lug, who swiftly grew proficient in every branch of skill

THE MYTHICAL HISTORY OF IRELAND

and knowledge, so that he became known as the Ioldánach (*Ildāna*), 'Master of all Arts.' He threw in his lot with his father's people, and organised the Tuatha Dé Danann for a great struggle. Incidentally, too, he obtained, as a blood-fine for the murder of his father at the hands of three grandsons of Ogma, the principal magic treasures of the world. The story of their quest is told in the romance of 'The Fate of the Children of Tuireann,' one of the famous 'Three Sorrowful Stories of Erin.'[1]

Thus, by the time the Fomorach had completed their seven years of preparation, the Tuatha Dé Danann were also ready for battle. Goibniu, the god of Smithcraft, had forged them magic weapons, while Diancecht, the god of Medicine, had made a magic well whose water healed the wounded and brought the slain to life. But this well was discovered by the spies of the Fomorach, and a party of them went to it secretly and filled it with stones.

After a few desultory duels, the great fight began on the plain of Carrowmore, near Sligo, the site, no doubt, of some prehistoric battle, the memorials of which still form the finest collection

[1] Translated by Eugene O'Curry, and published in vol. iv. of *Atlantis*.

of rude stone monuments in the world, with the one exception of Carnac.[1] It is called Moytura the Northern—to distinguish it from the other *Mag Tuireadh* further to the south. Great chiefs fell on either side. Ogma killed Indech, the son of the goddess Domnu, while Balor, the Fomor whose eye shot death, slew Nuada, the King of the Tuatha Dé Danann. But Lug turned the fortunes of the fray. With a carefully prepared magic sling-stone he blinded the terrible Balor and, at the fall of their principal champion, the Fomorach lost heart, and the Tuatha Dé Danann drove them back headlong to the sea. Bress himself was captured, and the rule of the Giants broken for ever.

But the power of the Tuatha Dé Danann was itself on the wane. They would seem, indeed, to have come to Ireland only to prepare the way for men, who were themselves issuant, according to the universal Celtic tradition, from the same progenitor and country as the gods.

In the Other World dwelt Bilé and Ith, deities of the dead. From their watch-tower they could look over the earth and see its various regions. Till now they had not noticed Ireland—perhaps on account of its slow and gradual growth—but

[1] Fergusson, *Rude Stone Monuments*, pp. 180, etc.

at last Ith, on a clear winter's night, descried it. Full of curiosity, he started on a tour of inspection and landed at the mouth of the Kenmare River. Journeying northwards, he came, with his followers, upon the Tuatha Dé Danann, who were in council at a spot near Londonderry still called Grianan Aileach to choose a new king.

Three sons of Ogma were the candidates—Mac Cuill, Mac Cecht, and Mac Gréine. Unable to come to a decision, the Tuatha Dé Danann called upon the stranger to arbitrate. He could not, or would not, do so; and, indeed, his whole attitude seemed so suspicious that the gods decided to kill him. This they did, but spared his followers, who returned to their own country, calling for vengeance.

Milé, the son of Bilé, was not slow in answering their appeal. He started for Ireland with his eight sons and their followers, and arrived there upon that same mysterious First of May on which both Partholon and the Tuatha Dé Danann themselves had first come to Ireland.

Marching through the country towards Tara, they met in succession three eponymous goddesses of the country, wives of Mac Cuill, Mac Cecht, and Mac Gréine. Their names were Banba, Fotla, and Eriu. Each in turn demanded of Amergin, the druid of the Milesians—as these first legendary Irish Celts are called—that, in the event of their success, the island should be called after her. Amergin promised it to them all, but, as Eriu asked last, it is her name (in the genitive case of 'Erinn') which has survived. The legend probably crystallizes what are said to have been the three first names of Ireland.

Soon they came to the capital and called the Tuatha Dé Danann to a parley. After some discussion it was decided that, as the Milesians were to blame for not having made due declaration of war before invading the country, their proper course was to retire to their ships and attempt a fresh landing. They anchored at 'nine green waves'' distance from the shore, and the Tuatha Dé Danann, ranged upon the beach, prepared druidical spells to prevent their approaching nearer.

Manannán, son of the Sea, waved his magic mantle and shook an off-shore wind straight into their teeth. But Amergin had powerful spells of his own. By incantations which have come down to us, and which are said to be the oldest Irish literary records, he propitiated both the Earth and the Sea, divinities more ancient and more powerful than any anthropomorphic gods, and in

THE MYTHICAL HISTORY OF IRELAND

the end a remnant of the Milesians came safely to shore in the estuary of the Boyne.

In two successive battles they defeated the Tuatha Dé Danann, whose three kings fell at the hands of the three surviving sons of Mílé. Disheartened, the gods yielded to the hardly less divine ancestors of the Gaels. A treaty of peace was, however, made with them, by which, in return for their surrender of the soil, they were to receive worship and sacrifice. Thus began religion in Ireland.

Driven from upper earth, they sought for new homes. Some withdrew to a Western Paradise—that Elysium of the Celts called Avallon by the Briton, and by many poetic names by the Gael. Others found safe seclusion in underground dwellings marked by barrows or hillocks. From these *sídhe*, as they are called, they took a new name, that of *Aes Sídhe*, 'Race of the Fairy Mounds,' and it is by this title, sometimes shortened to 'The Sídhe' (*Shee*), that the Irish peasantry of to-day call the fairies. The 'banshee' of popular story is none other than the *bean-sídhe*, the 'fairy woman,' the dethroned goddess of the Goidelic mythology.

CHAPTER V

THE MYTHICAL HISTORY OF BRITAIN

'WHEN Britain first, at Heaven's command, arose from out the azure main,' her name was *Clas Myrddin*, that is, the Place, or Enclosure, of Merlin. In later days, she became known as 'the Honey Isle of Beli,'[1] and it was not until safely occupied by mankind that she took her present designation, from Prydain, son of Aedd the Great, who first established settled government. All this is told us by a Welsh Triad, and it is from such fragmentary sources that we glean the mythical history of our island.

With these relics we must make what we can; for the work has not been done for us in the way that it was done by the mediaeval monkish annalists for Ireland. We find our data scattered through old bardic poems and romances, and in pseudo-hagiologies and hardly less apocryphal

---

[1] Beli seems to have been sometimes associated in Welsh legend with the sea, which was called the 'drink of Beli,' and its waves 'Beli's cattle.'

histories. Yet, without perhaps using more freedom with our materials than an early writer would have done, we can piece them together, and find in them roughly the same story as that of Ireland—the subjugation of the land by friendly gods for the subsequent use of men.

The greatest bulk of ancient British myth is found in the Mabinogion—more correctly, the Four Branches of the Mabinogi. These tales evidently consist of fragments of varying myths pieced together to make a cycle, and Professor Anwyl[1] has endeavoured with much learning to trace out and disentangle the original legends. But in the form in which the Welsh writer has fixed them, they show a gradual supersession of other deities by the gods who more especially represent human culture.

The first of the Four Branches deals with the leading incidents in the life of Pwyll: how he became a king in Annwn, the Other World of the Welsh; how, by a clever trick, he won his bride Rhiannon; the birth of their son Prydéri, and his theft by mysterious powers; the punishment incurred by Rhiannon on the false charge of having eaten him; and his recovery and restoration upon the night of the First of May.

In the second 'Branch' we find Prydéri, grown

[1] See a series of articles in the *Zeitschrift für Celtische Philologie*.

up and married to a wife called Kicva, as the guest of Brân, son of Llŷr, at Harlech. Matholwch, King of Ireland, arrives with a fleet to request the hand of Brân's sister, Branwen of the Fair Bosom. It is granted, and Branwen sails to Ireland. But, later on, news comes that she is being badly treated by her husband, and Brân goes with an army to avenge her. There is parley, submission, treachery, and battle, out of which, after the slaughter of all the Irish, only seven of Brân's host remain—Prydéri, Manawyddan, the bard Taliesin, and four others of less known mythic fame. Brân himself is wounded in the foot with a poisoned spear, and in his agony orders the others to cut off his head and carry it to 'the White Mount in London,' by which Tower Hill is believed to have been meant. They were eighty-seven years upon the way, cheered all the while by the singing of the Three Birds of Rhiannon, whose music was so sweet that it would recall the dead to life, and by the agreeable conversation of Brân's severed head. But at last they reached the end of their journey, and buried the head with its face turned towards France, watching that no foreign foe came to Britain. And here it reposed until Arthur disinterred it, scorning, in his pride of heart, to 'hold the island otherwise than by valour,' a rash act of which the Saxon conquest was the result.

The third Mabinogi recounts the further adventures of Manawyddan, who married the apparently old, but no doubt ever youthful, Rhiannon, mother of his friend Prydéri, and of Prydéri himself and his wife Kicva. During their absence in Ireland their kinsmen had all been slain by Caswallawn, a son of Beli, and their kingdom taken from them by the Children of Dôn. The four fugitives were compelled to live a homeless nomadic life, and it is the 'spiriting away' by magic of Rhiannon and Prydéri and their recovery by the craft of Manawyddan which forms the subject of the tale.

With the fourth 'Branch' the Children of Dôn come into a prominence which they keep to the end. They are shown as dwelling together at Caer Dathyl, an unidentified spot in the mountains of Carnarvonshire, and ruled over by Mâth, Dôn's brother. There are two chief incidents of the story. The first tells of the birth of the twin sons of Gwydion's sister, Arianrod—Dylan, apparently a marine deity,[1] who, as soon as he was

[1] Professor Rhŷs is inclined to see in him a deity of Darkness, opposed to the god of Light, *Hibbert Lectures*, p. 387. See in this connection p. 32 of the present book.

born, disappeared into the sea, where he swam as well as any fish, and Lleu, who was fostered and brought up by Gwydion; the rage of Arianrod when she found her intrigue made public, and her refusal of name, arms, or a wife to her unwished-for son; the craft by which Gwydion obtained for him those three essentials of a man's life; the infidelity of the damsel whom Mâth and Gwydion had created for Lleu 'by charms and illusion' out of 'the blossoms of the oak, and the blossoms of the broom, and the blossoms of the meadow-sweet,' and his enchantment into an eagle by the cunning of her lover; the wanderings of Gwydion in search of his protégé, and his eventual recovery of him; and the vengeance taken by Lleu upon the man and by Gwydion upon the woman. The second relates the coming of pigs to Britain as a gift from Arawn, King of Annwn, to Prydéri; their fraudulent acquisition by Gwydion; the war which followed the theft; and the death of Prydéri through the superior strength and magic of the great son of Dôn.

These 'Four Branches of the Mabinogi' thus give a consecutive, if incomplete, history of some of the most important of the Brythonic gods. There are, however, other isolated legends from which we can add to the information they afford.

THE MYTHICAL HISTORY OF BRITAIN

We learn more of the details of Gwydion's struggles with his enemies. In his first attempts he seems to have been unfortunate. Trespassing upon Hades, he was caught by Pwyll and Prydéri, and imprisoned in a mysterious island called Caer Sidi. It was the sufferings he endured there which made him a poet, and any one who aspires to a similar gift may try to gain it, it is said, by sleeping out either upon the top of Cader Idris or under the Black Stone of the Arddu upon the side of Snowdon, for from that night of terrors he will return either inspired or mad.

But Gwydion escaped from his enemies, and we find him victorious in the strange conflict called *Cad Goddeu*, the 'Battle of the Trees.' His brother Amaethon and his nephew Lleu were with him, and they fought against Brân and Arawn. We learn from various traditions how the sons of Dôn 'changed the forms of the elementary trees and sedges' into warriors; how Gwydion overcame the magic power of Brân by guessing his name; and how, by the defeat of the powers of the Underworld, three boons were won for man—the dog, the deer, and some bird whose name is translated as 'lapwing.'

But now a fresh protagonist comes upon the scene—the famous Arthur, whose history and even existence have been involved in so much doubt. The word *Arthur*, of which several varying explanations have been attempted, is now held to have been originally *Artōrius*, a recognised Latin name found on inscriptions, and as *Artūrius* in Juvenal, which would make him a Romanised Briton who, like many others of his period, adopted a Latin designation. His political prominence, implied not only by the traditions which make him a supreme war-leader of the Britons, but also by the fact that he is described in a twelfth century Welsh MS. as Emperor (*amherawdyr*), while his contemporaries, however high in rank, are only princes (*gwledig*), may be due, as Professor Rhŷs has suggested,[1] to his having filled, after the withdrawal of the Romans, a position equivalent to their *Comes Britanniae*. But his legendary fame is hardly to be explained except upon the supposition that the fabled exploits of a god or gods perhaps of somewhat similar name have become confounded with his own, as seems to have also happened in the case of Dietrich von Bern (Theodoric the Goth) and the Gaulish Toutiŏrix. An inscription has been found at Beaucroissant, in the valley of the Isère, to Mercurius Artaios, while the name

[1] *Studies in the Arthurian Legend*, p. 7.

THE MYTHICAL HISTORY OF BRITAIN

Artio appears elsewhere within the limits of ancient Gaul as that of a goddess These names may have been derived from either of two Celtic roots, *ar*, meaning 'to plough,' which would suggest a deity or deities of agriculture, or *art*, signifying a bear, as an animal worshipped at some remote period in the history of the Celts. Probably we shall never know exactly what diverse local myths have been woven into the story of Arthur, but they would doubtless be of the kind usually attributed to those divine benefactors known as 'Culture Heroes,' and it is to be noted that, in the earliest accounts we have of him, his character and attributes are extremely like those of another culture hero, Gwydion son of Dôn.

Like Gwydion, he suffered imprisonment at the hands of his enemies. He 'was for three nights in the Castle of Oeth and Annoeth'—the gruesome structure of human bones built by Manawyddan son of Llŷr in Gower—'and three nights in the prison of (?) Wen Pendragon,[1] and three nights in the dark prison under the stone,' a Triad tells us. Like Gwydion, too, he went pig-stealing, but he was neither so lucky nor so

[1] Professor Anwyl suggests that this name may have been originally Uthr Bendragon, *i.e.* Brân. See p. 71.

crafty as his predecessor. When he had designs upon the swine of March son of Meirchion (the 'King Mark' of the romances) which Trystan was herding, he could not get, says another Triad, even one pig. But in the end he succeeded wholly. An old Welsh poem tells us of his 'Spoiling of Annwn' (*Preiddeu Annwn*)[1] and his capture of the magic cauldron of its King, though, like Brân himself when he went to Ireland, he brought back with him from his expedition only seven of the men who, at starting, had been 'thrice enough to fill Prydwen,' his ship.

But, having accomplished this, he seems to have had the other, and perhaps older, gods at his feet. Llûdd, according to Triads, was one of his Three Chief War Knights, and Arawn one of his Three Chief Counselling Knights. In the story of the hunting of the wild boar Twrch Trwyth, a quest in the course of which he acquired the 'Treasures of Britain,' he is served not only by Amaethon and Govannon, sons of Dôn, but also by the same Manawyddan who had been his gaoler and another whilom king in Hades, Gwyn son of Nûdd. This tale, like its similar in Gaelic myth, the 'Fate of the Children

[1] 'Book of Taliesin,' poem xxx., Skene, vol. i. p. 256.

THE MYTHICAL HISTORY OF BRITAIN

of Tuireann,' is a long one, and the reader is referred to Lady Guest's *Mabinogion* for the full story, which a good judge has acclaimed to be, 'saving the finest tales of the "Arabian Nights," the greatest romantic fairy tale the world has ever known.'[1] The pursuit of wondrous pigs seems to have been an important feature of Arthur's career. Besides the boar Trwyth, he assembled his hosts to capture a sow called Henwen, which led him through the length of Wales. Wherever she went she dropped the germs of wealth for Britain—three grains of wheat and three bees, a grain of barley, a little pig, and a grain of rye. But she left evils behind her as well, a wolf cub and an eaglet which caused trouble afterwards, as well as a kitten which grew up to be 'the Palug Cat,' famous as one of the 'Three Plagues of the Isle of Mona.'[2]

Of what may have been historical elements in his story, the Triads also take notice. We learn how Arthur and Medrawt raided each other's courts during the owner's absence, and that the battle of Camlan was one of the 'Three Frivolous

---

[1] Mr. Alfred Nutt, in his notes to his edition (1902) of Lady Guest's *Mabinogion*.

[2] This creature is also mentioned in an Arthurian poem in the twelfth century Black Book of Carmarthen.

Battles of Britain,' because during it the two antagonists thrice shared their forces, and that the usual 'Three' alone escaped from it, though Arthur himself is, in spite of the triadic convention, added as a fourth.

So he vanishes, passing to Avilion (Avallon), and the end of the divine age is also marked by the similar departure of his associate Myrddin, or Merlin, to an island beyond the sunset, accompanied by nine bards bearing with them those wondrous talismans, the Thirteen Treasures. Britain was now ready for her Britons.

In Gwlâd yr Hâv, the 'Land of Summer'—a name for the Brythonic Other World—dwelt the ancestors of the Cymry, ruled over by a divine hero called Hû Gadarn ('the Mighty'), and the time was ripe for their coming to our island.

Apparently we have a similar legend to the story of the conquest of Ireland from the Tuatha Dé Danann by the Milesians, though there is here no hint of fighting, it being, on the contrary, stated in a Triad that Hû obtained his dominion over Britain not by war and bloodshed, but by justice and peace. He instructed his people in the art of agriculture, divided them into federated tribes as a first step towards civil government, and laid the foundations of literature and history by the institution of bardism. He put a stop to disastrous floods by dragging out of the lake where it concealed itself the dragon-like monster which caused them, and, after the waters had subsided, he was the first to draw on British soil a furrow with a plough. Therefore he is called the first of the 'Three National Pillars of the Isle of Britain,' the second being the Prydain who gave her his name, while the third was the mythical legislator Dyvnwal Moelmud, 'who reduced to a system the laws, customs, maxims, and privileges appertaining to a country and nation.'

CHAPTER VI

THE HEROIC CYCLE OF ANCIENT ULSTER

In addition to the myths of the Tuatha Dé Danann, and the not less apocryphal stories of her early 'Milesian' kings, Ireland has evolved two heroic cycles. The completest, and in some ways the most interesting, of these deals with the palmy days of the then Kingdom of Ulster during the reign of Conchobar (*Conahar*) Mac Nessa, whom the early annalists place at about the beginning of the Christian era. But, precise as this statement sounds and vividly as the 'Champions of the Red Branch,' as King Conchobar's braves were called, are depicted for us by the story-tellers, there is probably little, if any, foundation of fact in their legends. We may discern in their genealogies and the stories of their births the clue to their real nature. Their chief figures draw descent from the Tuatha Dé Danann, and are twice described in the oldest manuscripts as 'terrestrial gods.' One may compare them with the divinely descended heroes of the Greeks.

The sagas, or romances, which make up the Ulster cycle are found mainly in three manuscripts, the Book of the Dun Cow and the Book of Leinster, both of which date from the beginning of the twelfth century, and the Yellow Book of Lecan, assigned to the end of the fourteenth. The longest and most important of them is known as the *Táin Bó Chuailgne* (the 'Cattle Raid of Cooley') the chief figure of which is the famous Cuchulainn, or Cuchullin, the son of Conchobar's sister Dechtiré by Lug of the Tuatha Dé Danann.

Cuchulainn, indeed, *fortissimus heros Scottorum*, is the real centre of the whole cycle. It is very doubtful whether he ever had actual existence. His attributes and adventures are of the type usually recorded of what are called 'solar heroes.' When in his full strength no one could look him in the face without blinking. The heat of his body melted snow and boiled water. It was *geis* ('taboo') to him to behold the sea. The antagonists whom he conquers are often suspiciously like mythological personifications of the dark shades of night.

He was first called Setanta, but it was while he was still quite a child that he changed his

MYTHOLOGY OF ANCIENT BRITAIN

name to *Cú Chulainn* ('Hound of Culann') as the result of an exploit in which he killed the watch-dog of the chief smith of Ulster, and afterwards acted as its substitute until another could be procured and trained.

Other stories of his youth tell how he assumed arms at the age of seven, and slew three champions who had set all the warriors of Ulster at defiance; how he travelled to Alba (Scotland) to learn the highest skill in arms from Scáthach, the Warrior-Witch who gave her name to the Isle of Skye; how he carried off his bride Emer (*Avair*) in the teeth of a host; and how, by success in a series of terrible tests, he gained the right to be called Head-Champion of Ulster.

But these isolated sagas are only external to the real core of the cycle, the *Táin Bó Chuailgne*. This is the story of a war which the other four kingdoms of Ireland—Meath, Munster, Leinster and Connaught—made upon Ulster at the bidding of Medb (*Maive*), the Amazon-Queen of the last-named province, to obtain possession of a magic bull called The Brown of Cualgne. Its interest lies in no promiscuous battles in which the deeds of an individual warrior are dwarfed by those of his compeers. For the mythic raid was undertaken at a time when all Conchobar's warriors

HEROIC CYCLE OF ANCIENT ULSTER

were lying under a strange magic weakness which incapacitated them from fighting. Anthropologists tend to see in this mysterious infirmity a distorted memory of the primitive custom of the *couvade*, and mythologists the helplessness of the gods of vegetation and agriculture during the winter, while the storytellers attribute it to a curse once laid upon Ulster by the goddess Macha. But when the land seemed most at its enemy's mercy, the heroic Cuchulainn, who for some unexplained reason was not subject to the same incapacity as his fellow-tribesmen, stood up to defend it single-handed. For three months he held the marches against all comers, fighting a fresh champion every day, and the story of the *Táin* consists mainly of a long series of duels in which exponents of every savage art of war or witchcraft are sent against him,—each to be defeated in his turn. Over this tremendous struggle hover the figures of the Tuatha Dé Danann. Lug, Cuchulainn's divine father, comes to heal his son's wounds, and the fierce Mórrígu, queen of battle, is moved to offer so unrivalled a hero her love. A short-lived pathos illumines the story in the tale of his combat with his old friend and sworn companion, Ferdiad, who, drugged with love and wine, had rashly pledged his word to take up the standing challenge. After a three days' duel, during which the courtesies exchanged between the two combatants are not excelled in any tale of mediaeval chivalry, Cuchulainn gives the death-blow to the foe who is still his friend. When he sees him at his feet, he bursts into passionate lament. 'It was all a game and a sport until Ferdiad came; the memory of this day will be like a cloud hanging over me for ever.' But the victory ended his perilous labours; for the men of Ulster, at last shaking off their weakness, came down and dispersed their enemies.

Other stories of the cycle tell of such episodes as Cuchulainn's unwitting slaying of his only son in single combat, an old Aryan *motif* which we find also in Teutonic and Persian myth, or his visit to the Celtic Other World, and his love adventure with Fand, the deserted wife of Manannán son of Lêr; until at last the mass of legends which make up a complete story of the hero's career are closed with the tragedy of his death upon the plain of Muirthemné.

It was planned by Medb with the sons and relations of the chiefs whom Cuchulainn had killed in battle, and no stone was left unturned to compass his downfall. Three witches who had been to Alba and Babylon to learn all the sorcery

of the world deceive him with magic shows, and
draw him out alone into the open; he is tricked
into breaking his *taboo* by eating the flesh of a
dog—his name-sake, says the story, but perhaps
also his *totem*; satirists demand his favourite
weapons, threatening to lampoon his family if he
refuses; and thus, stripped of material and super-
natural aid, he is attacked by overwhelming
numbers. But, though signs and portents an-
nounce his doom, there is no 'shadow of chang-
ing' in the hero's indomitable heart. Wounded
to the death, he binds himself with his belt to a
pillar-stone, so that he may die standing; and,
even after he has drawn his last breath, his
sword, falling from his grasp, chops off the hand
of the enemy who has come to take his head.

Out of the seventy-six stories of the Ulster
cycle which have come down to us, no less than
sixteen are personal to Cuchulainn. But the other
heroes are not altogether forgotten, though their
lists are comparatively short. Most of these tales
have been already translated, and, taken together,
they form a narrative which is almost epic in its
completeness and interest.[1]

---

[1] A list of the tales, extant and lost, of the Ulster Cycle will
be found as Appendix I. of Miss Eleanor Hull's *Cuchullin Saga*,
London, 1898.

MYTHOLOGY OF ANCIENT BRITAIN

Probably its growth was gradual, and spread over a considerable time. Some of the redactors, too, have evidently had a hand in recasting the pagan myths of Ulster for the purposes of Christian edification. We are told with startling inconsistency how Cuchulainn, going to his last fight, heard the angels hymning in Heaven, confessed the true faith, and was cheered by the certainty of salvation. The 'Tragical Death of Conchobar,' in the Book of the Dun Cow relates how that king died of wrath and sorrow at learning of the Passion of Christ. Another story from the same source, entitled 'The Phantom Chariot,' shows us Cuchulainn, conjured from the dead by St. Patrick, testifying to the truth of Christianity before an Irish king. But such interpolations do not affect the real matter of the cycle, which presents us with a picture of the Celts of Ireland at an age perhaps contemporary with Caesar's invasion of her sister isle of Britain.

CHAPTER VII

THE FENIAN, OR OSSIANIC, SAGAS

THE second of the two Gaelic heroic cycles presents certain striking contrasts to the first. It depicts a quite different stage of human culture; for, while the Ulster stories deal with chariot-driving chiefs ruling over settled communities from fortified dúns, the Fenian sagas mirror, under a faint disguise, the lives of nomad hunters in primeval woods. The especial possession, not of any one tribal community, but of the folk, it is common to the two Goidelic countries, being as native to Scotland as to Ireland. Moreover, it has the distinction, unique among early literatures, of being still a living tradition. So firmly rooted are the memories of Finn and his heroes in the minds of the Gaelic peasantry that there is a proverb to the effect that if the Fenians found that they had not been spoken of for a day, they would rise from the dead.

MYTHOLOGY OF ANCIENT BRITAIN

It may be well here to remove a few possible misconceptions concerning these sagas and their heroes. The word 'Fenian' in popular parlance is applied to certain political agitators of recent notoriety. But those 'Fenians' merely assumed their title from the tradition that the original Fianna (*Fēna*) were a band of patriots sworn to the defence of Ireland. With regard, too, to the second title of 'Ossianic' which the romances and poems which make up the cycle bear, it must not be taken that the Fenian hero Ossian was their author, an idea perhaps suggested by the prose-poem of James MacPherson, which, though doubtless founded upon genuine Gaelic material, was almost certainly that writer's own composition. Some of the poetical pieces are, indeed, rightly or wrongly attributed to Ossian, as some are to Finn himself, but the bulk of the poems and all the prose tales are, like the sagas of the Ulster cycle, by unknown authors. A few of them are found in the earliest Irish manuscripts, but there has been a continuous stream of literary treatment of them, and they have also been handed down as folk-tales by oral tradition.

The cycle as a whole deals with the history and adventures of a band of warriors who are described as having formed a standing force, in the pay of

THE FENIAN OR OSSIANIC SAGAS

the High Kings of Tara, to protect Ireland, both from internal trouble and foreign invasion. The early annalists were quite certain of their historical reality, and dated their existence as a body from 300 B.C. to 284 A.D., while even so late and sound a scholar as Eugene O'Curry gave his opinion that Finn himself was as undoubtedly historical a character as Julius Caesar.

Modern Celtic students, however, tend to reverse this view. The name Fionn or Finn, meaning 'white,' or 'fair,' appears elsewhere as that of a mythical ancestor of the Gaels. His father's name Cumhal (*Coul*), according to Professor Rhŷs, is identical with Cămŭlos and the German *Himmel* (Heaven). The same writer is inclined to equate Fionn mac Cumhail with Gwyn ab Nûdd, a 'White son of Sky' who, we have seen, was a British god of the Other World, and, afterwards, king of the Welsh fairies.[1] But there may have been a historical nucleus of the Fenian cycle into which myths of gods and heroes became incorporated.

This possible starting-point would show us a roving band of picked soldiers, following the chase in summer, quartered on the towns in

[1] Rhŷs, *Hibbert Lectures*, pp. 178, 179. But these identifications are contested.

winter, but always ready to march, at the bidding of the High King of Ireland, to quell any disturbance or to meet any foreign foe. For a time all goes smoothly. But at last their exactions rouse the people against them, and their pride affronts the king. Dissensions leading to internecine strife break out among themselves, and, taking advantage of these, king and people make common cause and destroy them.

In the romances, this seed of decay is sown before the birth of Finn. His father Cumhal banishes Goll (*Gaul*), head of the powerful clan of Morna. Goll goes into exile but returns, defeats and kills Cumhal, and disperses the clan of Baoisgne (*Baskin*), his tribe. But Cumhal's posthumous son is brought up in secret, is trained to manly feats, and, as the reward of a deed of prowess, is called upon by the High King to claim a boon. 'I ask only for my lawful inheritance,' says the youth, and tells his name. The king insists upon Goll admitting Finn's rights, and so he becomes leader of the Fenians. But, in the end, the smouldering enmity breaks out, and, after the death of Goll, the rest of the clan of Morna go over to the High King of Ireland—Cairbré, son of the Cormac who had restored Finn to his heritage. The disastrous battle of Gavra is fought, in which

THE FENIAN OR OSSIANIC SAGAS

Cairbré himself falls, while the Fenians are practically annihilated.

But attached to this possibly historical nucleus is a mass of tales which may well have once been independent of it. Their actors are the principal figures of the Fenian chivalry—Fionn (*Finn*) himself, his son Oisin (*Ossian*), and his grandson Osgur (*Oscar*); his cousin Caoilte (*Kylta*), swiftest-footed of men, and his nephew Diarmait (*Dermat*), the lover of women; with the proud Goll and his braggart brother Conan, leaders of the clan of Morna. They consist of wonderful adventures, sometimes with invaders from abroad, but oftener upon 'perilous seas' and 'in faery lands forlorn' with wild beasts, giants, witches and wizards, and the Tuatha Dé Danann themselves. The Fenians have the freedom of the *sidhe*, the palaces under the fairy hills, and help this god or that against his fellows. Even Bodb Derg (Red Bove) a son of the Dagda, gives his daughter to Finn and sends his son to enlist with the Fenians. The culmination of these exploits is related in the tale called *Cath Finntraighe*[1] (the Battle of Ventry), in which Dairé Donn, the High King of the World, leads all his vassals against Ireland,

---

[1] Translated by Professor Kuno Meyer, in vol. i. of *Anecdota Oxoniensia*, 1882.

and is defeated by the joint efforts of the Fenians and the Tuatha Dé Danann.

Ossian takes, of course, a prominent part in the stories which are so much associated with his name. But he is especially connected with what might be called the 'post-Fenian ballads,' in which the heroic deeds of Finn and his men are told in the form of dialogues between Ossian and St. Patrick. They hinge upon the legend that Ossian escaped the fate of the rest of his kin by being taken to *Tir nan Og*, the 'Land of Youth,'—the Celtic Paradise of old and the Celtic Fairyland of to-day—by the fairy, or goddess, Niamh (*Neeave*), daughter of Manannán mac Lir. Here he enjoyed three hundred years of divine youth, while time changed the face of the world outside. In the end he longs to see his own country again, and Niamh mounts him upon a magic horse, warning him not to put foot upon earthly soil. But his saddle-girth breaks, Ossian falls to earth, and rises up, a blind old man, stripped of the gifts of the gods.

The ballad 'Dialogues' recite the arguments held between the saint and the hero. Saint Patrick presses the new creed and culture upon his unwilling guest, who answers him with passionate laments for the days that are dead. Patrick tells

THE FENIAN OR OSSIANIC SAGAS

of God and the Angels, Ossian retorts with tales of Finn and the Fenians. It is the clash of two aspects of life, the heathen ideal of joy and strength, and the Christian ideal of service and sacrifice. 'I will tell you a little story about Finn,' replies Ossian to the saint's praises of the heaven of the elect, and relates some heroic exploit of chase or war. Nor is he more ready to listen to Patrick's exhortations to repent and weep over his pagan past. 'I will weep my fill,' he answers, 'but not for God, but because Finn and the Fenians are no longer alive.'

CHAPTER VIII

THE ARTHURIAN LEGEND

But the Gaelic myths, vital as they are, have yet caused no echo of themselves in the literatures of the outside world. This distinction has been left for the legendary tales of the Britons. The Norman minstrels found the stories which they heard from their Welsh confrères so much to their liking that they readily adopted them, and spread them from camp to camp and from court to court, wherever their dominant race held sway. Perhaps the finer qualities of Celtic romance made especial appeal to that new fashion of 'chivalry' which was growing up under the fosterage of poetry and romance by noble ladies. At any rate the *Matière de Bretagne*, as the stories of the British gods and heroes, and especially of Arthur, were called, came to be the leading source of poetic inspiration on the Continent. The whole vast Arthurian literature has its origin in British Celtic mythology.

THE ARTHURIAN LEGEND

We find the names of its chief characters, and can trace the nucleus of their stories, in Welsh songs and tales older than the earliest outburst of Arthurian romance in Europe. Arthur himself has, as we have tried to show in a previous chapter, several of the attributes and adventures of Gwydion son of Dôn, while the figures most closely connected with his story bear striking resemblance to the characters which surround Gwydion in the fourth 'branch' of the Mabinogi,[1] a result probably due to the same type of myth having been current in different localities and associated in different districts with different names. Arianrod, who is said to have been the wife of a little-known and perhaps superseded and half-forgotten Sky-god called Nwyvre ('Space'), seems to be represented in Arthur's story by Gwyar, the consort of the Heaven-god Llûdd, and from comparison with later romance we may fairly assume that Gwyar was also Arthur's sister. In Gwalchmai and Medrawt, the good and evil brothers born of their union, we shall probably be right in recognising similar characters to Arianrod's sons, the gods of light and darkness, Lleu (Llew) and Dylan. This body of myth has passed down

---

[1] See Rhŷs, *Studies in the Arthurian Legend*, chap. i. 'Arthur, Historical and Mythical.'

almost intact into the mediaeval Arthurian cycle. The wife of King Lot (Llûdd) is sister to Arthur; Lleu's counterpart, Gwalchmai,[1] appears as Sir Gawaine, certain descriptions of whom in Malory's *Morte Darthur* are hardly comprehensible except as a misunderstood fragment of a mythology in which he appeared as a 'solar hero'; Medrawt has scarcely changed at all, either in name or character, in becoming Sir Mordred; while the stately figure of Mâth, ruler of the children of Dôn, is paralleled by the majestic Merlin, who watches over, and even dares to rebuke, his protégé, Arthur.

We are upon uncertain ground, however, in attempting to discover in the Arthurian cycle the other personages of the Mabinogian stories. Professor Rhŷs, in his *Studies in the Arthurian Legend* (1891), has devoted great ingenuity and learning to this task, but his identifications of Pwyll, of Rhiannon, of Prydéri, of Arawn, of Gwyn, and of Amaethon with characters in the mediaeval romances, whatever may happen to them in the future, cannot at present be considered as otherwise than hazardous. The transformations of Brân seem less open to doubt.

---

[1] In Welsh legend, Gwalchmai (the 'Hawk of May') has a brother, Gwalchaved (the 'Hawk of Summer'), whose name is the original of 'Galahad.'

THE ARTHURIAN LEGEND

The name of King Brandegore may probably be resolved into Brân of Gower, and of Sir Brandiles into Brân of Gwales (Gresholm Island); he is perhaps King Ban of Benwyk, and Bron, who brought the Grail to Britain; as Balan, he is brought into contact with Balin, who seems to be the Gallo-British Bĕlĕnos; while Uther Pendragon himself may have been originally Brân's 'Wonderful Head' (*Uthr Ben*) which lived for eighty-seven years after it had been severed from its body. But there can be little question as to other personages who surround Arthur both in the earlier and later legends. Myrddin as Merlin; March as King Mark; Gwalchaved as Sir Galahad; Kai as Sir Kay; and Gwenhwyvar as Guinevere have obviously been directly taken over from Welsh story.

But here we are confronted with a notable exception. It is of Sir Lancelot, King Arthur's peerless knight and the lover of Queen Guinevere, that no trace can be found in earlier legend. He is not heard of till the latter part of the twelfth century, when he appears as a knight who was stolen in infancy, and brought up by a water-fairy (whence his title of *Du Lac*),[1] but thenceforward he supersedes in popularity all the others of the

[1] See Miss J. L. Weston's *The Legend of Sir Lancelot Du Lac*. London, 1901.

Table Round. In his rôle of the lover of the Queen, he pushes his way into, and shatters, the older traditions. According to early story it was Melwas, the Cornish equivalent of the Welsh Gwyn ab Nûdd, who stole Gwenhwyvar, and Arthur himself who recaptured her. But in the *Morte Darthur*, though Melwas, whose name has become 'Sir Meliagraunce,' is still the abductor of Queen Guinevere, it is Sir Lancelot who appears as her deliverer. Nor can Sir Mordred, or Medrawt, another traditional rival of Arthur's, hold his own against the new-comer.

Probably we shall never solve this mystery. Some literary or social fashion of which all record is lost may have dictated Lancelot's prominence. It matters less, as it is not the core and centre of the Arthurian legend. What has given the cycle its enduring interest, as testified by its attraction for author, artist, and composer down to the present day, is not the somewhat commonplace love of Lancelot and the Queen, but the mystical quest of the Holy Grail. And here we can clearly trace the direct evolution of the Arthurian legend from the myths of the Celts.[1]

[1] The chief authorities for the study of the Grail legend in its relation to Celtic myth are Professor Rhŷs's *Studies in the Arthurian Legend* and Mr. Alfred Nutt's *Studies on the Legend of the Holy Grail*.

THE ARTHURIAN LEGEND

Both in Gaelic and British mythology, prominence is given to a cauldron which has wondrous talismanic virtues. It was one of the four chief treasures brought by the Tuatha Dé Danann to Ireland; Cuchulainn captured it from the god Mider, when he stormed his stronghold in the Isle of Man; and it reappears in the Fenian stories. Its especial property in these myths was that of miraculous food-providing—all the men in the world, we are told, could be fed from it—and in this quality we find it on British ground as the basket of Gwyddneu Garanhir. But certain other such vessels of Brythonic myth were endowed with different, and less material, virtues. A magic cauldron given by Brân son of Llŷr to Matholwch, the husband of his sister Branwen, would restore the dead to life; in her cauldron of Inspiration and Science, the goddess Kerridwen brewed a drink of prophecy; while from the cauldron of the giant Ogyrvan, the father of Gwenhwyvar, the three Muses had been born.

In what is perhaps the latest of all these varying legends, the qualities of the previous cauldrons have been brought together to form the trophy which Arthur, in the early Welsh poem called 'The Spoiling of Annwn,' (see p. 50) is represented as having captured from the Other World King.

MYTHOLOGY OF ANCIENT BRITAIN

'Is it not the cauldron of the Chief of Annwn?' 'What is its fashion?' asks the bard Taliesin, and he goes on to describe it as rimmed with pearls, and gently warmed by the breath of nine maidens. 'It will not cook the food of a coward or one forsworn,' he continues, which allows us to assume that, like such vessels as the Dagda's cauldron or the basket of Gwyddneu Garanhir, it would provide generously for the brave and truthful. It was kept in a square fortress surrounded by the sea, and called by various names, such as the Revolving Castle (*Caer Sidi*), the Underworld (*Uffern*), the Four-cornered Castle (*Caer Pedryvan*), the Castle of (?) Revelry (*Caer Vedwyd*), the (?) Kingly Castle (*Caer Rigor*), the Glass Castle (*Caer Wydyr*), and the Castle of (?) Riches (*Caer Golud*). This stronghold, ruled over by Pwyll and Prydéri, is represented as spinning round with such velocity that it was almost impossible to enter it, and was in pitch-darkness save for a twilight made by the lamp burning before its gate, but its inhabitants, who were exempt from old age and disease, led lives of revelry, quaffing the bright wine. Evidently, as may be ascertained from comparison with similar myths, it stood for the Other World, as conceived by the Celts.

This cauldron of pagan myth has altered

THE ARTHURIAN LEGEND

strangely little in passing down through the centuries to become the Holy Grail which had been filled by Joseph of Arimathea with Christ's Blood. It is still kept in a mysterious castle by a mysterious king. In Malory's *Morte Darthur* this king is called Pelles, a name strangely like that of the Welsh Pwyll, and though in other versions of the Grail story, taken perhaps from variant British myths, the keeper of the mystic vessel bears a different name, he always seems to be one of the rulers of the Other World, whether he be called Bron (Brân), or Peleur (? Prydéri), or Goon (? Gwyn), or the Rich Fisher, in whom Professor Rhŷs recognises Gwyddneu Garanhir.[1] It still retains in essence the qualities of 'the cauldron of the Chief of Annwn.' The savage cooking-pot which would refuse to serve a coward or perjurer with food, has been only refined, not altered, in becoming the heavenly vessel which could not be seen by sinners, while the older idea is still retained in the account of how, when it appeared, it filled the hall with sweet savours, while every knight saw before him on the table the food he loved best. Like its pagan prototype, it cured wounds and sickness, and no one could grow old while in its presence. Though, too, the

[1] *Arthurian Legend*, pp. 315-317.

place in which it was kept is but vaguely pictured by Sir Thomas Malory, the thirteenth century Norman-French romance called the *Seint Greal*[1] preserves all the characteristics which most strike us in Taliesin's poem. It is surrounded by a great water; it revolves more swiftly than the wind; and its garrison shoot so stoutly that no armour can repel their shafts, which explains why, of the men that accompanied Arthur, 'except seven, none returned from Caer Sidi.'

'The kingdom of heaven suffereth violence, and the violent take it by force'; this is the spiritualised meaning of the Celtic myth, and in this has lain the lasting inspiration of the story which attracted Milton so strongly that it was almost by chance that we did not have from him a *King Arthur* instead of *Paradise Lost*. In our own times it has enchanted the imagination of Tennyson, while Swinburne, Morris, and Matthew Arnold have also borne witness to the poetic value of a tradition which is as national to Britain as the Veda to India, or her epic poems to Greece.

[1] Edited and translated by the Rev. Robert Williams, M.A. London, 1876.

CHRONOLOGICAL SYLLABUS

HISTORICAL.—Arrival in Britain of the earliest Celts (Goidels) about 1000-500 B.C.—Brythons and Belgæ, coming over during the 2nd and 3rd centuries B.C., largely supplant the Goidels—Belgic settlers still crossing over from Gaul in the time of Julius Caesar, who made his first invasion 55 B.C.—Britain declared a Roman province under Claudius A.D. 43—Abandoned under Honorius A.D. 410—*Druidism* forbidden to Roman citizens under Tiberius (*reigned* A.D. 14-37) and its complete suppression ordered by Claudius (*reigned* A.D. 41-54)—The chief stronghold of the Druids in Britain destroyed under Suetonius Paulinus, A.D. 61—*Christianity*, introduced under the Roman rule, makes gradual headway—Gildas, writing in the sixth century, describes paganism as extinct in civilised Britain—Era of St. Patrick in Ireland, fifth century—St. Columba carries the gospel to the Northern Picts, sixth century.

TRADITIONAL.—Fictitious dates assigned by the Irish compilers of pseudo-annals for all the mythical eras and events—Possibly authentic may be the placing of the heroic age of Ulster in the first century A.D. and the epoch of the Fenians in the second and third—British gods enrolled as early kings by Geoffrey of Monmouth or made the founders of powerful or saintly families by Welsh genealogists—The historic Arthur may have lived in the fifth-sixth centuries.

LITERARY.—The sixth century A.D. is the traditional period of the bards Myrddin, Aneurin, Taliesin, and Llywarch Hên, poems ascribed to whom are found in the Welsh mediaeval

MYTHOLOGY OF ANCIENT BRITAIN

MSS., while Irish legend asserts that the *Táin Bó Chuailgne* was first reduced to writing in the seventh—Gradual accumulation of Irish and Welsh mythical sagas, including the Four Branches of the Mabinogi, eighth-eleventh—The Irish Book of the Dun Cow and Book of Leinster and the Welsh Black Book of Carmarthen, compiled during the twelfth ; the Welsh Books of Aneurin and of Taliesin during the thirteenth ; and the Irish Book of Ballymote and the Yellow Book of Lecan and the Welsh Red Book of Hergest during the fourteenth—About 1136 Geoffrey of Monmouth finished his *Historia Britonum,* and during this century and the one following British mythical and heroic legend was moulded into the Continental Arthurian romances—About 1470 Sir Thomas Malory composed his *Morte Darthur* from French sources—The working-up of Gaelic traditional material ended probably in the middle of the eighteenth century—James MacPherson produced his pseudo-Ossianic 'epics,' 1760-63—In 1838-49 Lady Charlotte Guest published her *Mabinogion,* and from this date the renaissance of Celtic study and inspiration may be said to have commenced.

SELECTED BOOKS BEARING ON CELTIC MYTHOLOGY

To give in the space that can be spared any adequate list of books dealing with the wide subject of Celtic Mythology would be impossible. The reader interested in the matter can hardly do better than consult Nos. 1, 3, 4, 6, 8, 11, and 14 of the *Popular Studies in Mythology Romance and Folklore*, published by Mr. Nutt. In these sixpenny booklets he will find, not only scholarly introductions to the Gaelic Tuatha Dé Danann, Cuchulainn and Ossianic cycles, the Welsh Mabinogion, and the Arthurian legend, but also bibliographical appendices pointing out with sufficient fulness the chief works to consult. Should he be content with a more superficial survey, he might obtain it from the present writer's *The Mythology of the British Islands*, London, 1905, which aimed at giving, in a popular manner, sketches of the different cycles, and retellings of their principal stories, with a certain amount of explanatory comment.

For the stories themselves, he may turn to Lady Gregory's *Cuchulain of Muirthemne*, London, 1902, and *Gods and Fighting Men*, London, 1904, which give in attractive paraphrase all of the most important legends dealing with the Red Branch of Ulster and with the Tuatha Dé Danann and the Fenians. More exact translations of the Ulster romances will be found in Miss E. Hull's *The Cuchullin Saga in Irish Literature*, London, 1898; in Monsieur H. d'Arbois de Jubainville's *L'Épopée Celtique en Irlande*, Paris, 1892 (vol. v. of the 'Cours de Littérature Celtique'); and in Miss

MYTHOLOGY OF ANCIENT BRITAIN

W. L. Faraday's *The Cattle Raid of Cualnge*, London, 1904. The Fenian sagas are best studied in the six volumes of the *Transactions of the Ossianic Society*, Dublin, 1854-61; in Mr. S. H. O'Grady's *Silva Gadelica*, London, 1892; and in the Rev. J. G. Campbell's *The Fians*, London, 1891 (vol. iv. of 'Waifs and Strays of Celtic Tradition'). Lady Charlotte Guest's *Mabinogion* can now be obtained in several cheap editions, while Monsieur J. Loth's translation, *Les Mabinogion*, Paris, 1889, forms vols. iii. and iv. of the 'Cours de Littérature Celtique.'

Critical studies on the subject in handy form are as yet few. We may mention De Jubainville's *Le Cycle Mythologique Irlandais et la Mythologie Celtique*, Paris, 1884 (vol. ii. of the 'Cours'), translated by Mr. R. I. Best as *The Irish Mythological Cycle and Celtic Mythology*, Dublin, 1903; Professor J. Rhŷs's *Lectures on the Origin and Growth of Religion as Illustrated by Celtic Heathendom* (*The Hibbert Lectures for 1886*), London, 3rd edit., 1898, with their sequel, *Studies in the Arthurian Legend*, Oxford, 1891; and Mr. Alfred Nutt's *The Voyage of Bran, son of Febal*, 2 vols., London, 1895-97. The results of more recent, and current, research will be found in special publications, such as the volumes of the *Irish Texts Society*, and the numbers of the *Revue Celtique*, the *Zeitschrift für Celtische Philologie*, and the *Transactions of the Cymmrodorion Society*.

DATE DUE

WITHDRAWN

47912257
BL980 .G756 1975
SQUIRE CHARLES
MYTHOLOGY OF ANCIENT
BRITAIN AND IRELAND

MONTGOMERY COLLEGE LIBRARIES
0 0000 00406589 2